D1283644

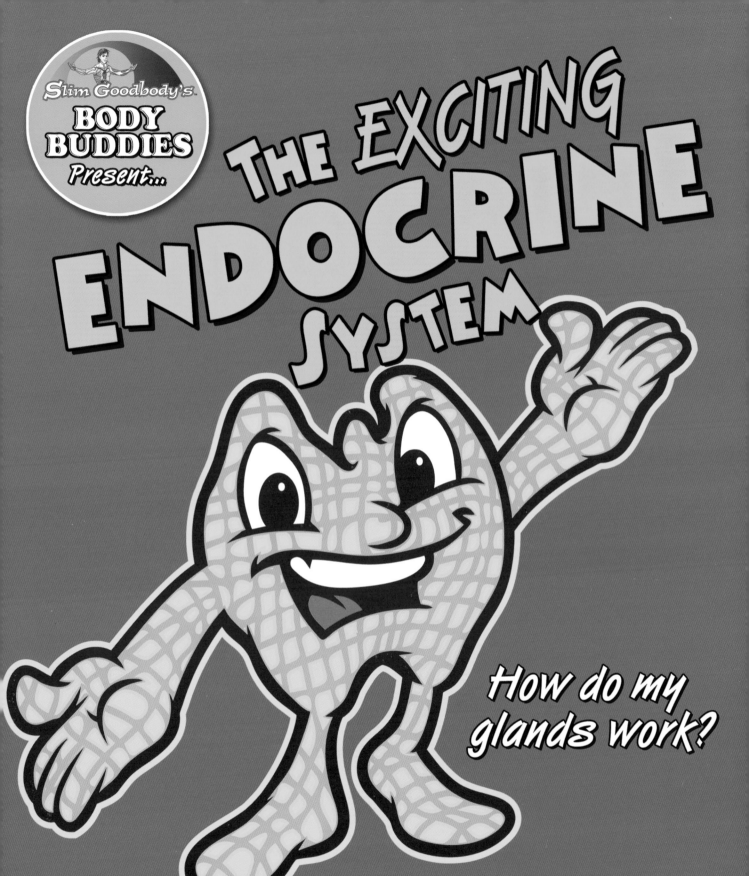

Slim Goodbody's BODY BUDDIES Present...

THE EXCITING ENDOCRINE SYSTEM

How do my glands work?

CRABTREE
Publishing Company
www.crabtreebooks.com

Crabtree Publishing Company
www.crabtreebooks.com

Series Development, Writing, and Packaging:
  John Burstein Slim Goodbody Corp.
Medical Reviewer:
  Christine S. Burstein, RN, MSN, FNP
Designer: Tammy West, Westgraphix
Project coordinator: Robert Walker
Editors: Mark Sachner, Water Buffalo Books
  Molly Aloian
Proofreader: Adrianna Morganelli
Production coordinator: Katherine Berti
Prepress technicians: Rosie Gowsell,
  Katherine Berti, Ken Wright
Squirt Character Design and Illustration:
  Mike Ray, Ink Tycoon
Medical Illustrations: Colette Sands,
  Render Ranch, and Mike Ray

Picture credits:
© istockphoto: p. 9a, 9b, 15b, 27
© Shutterstock: p. 19b
© Slim Goodbody: cover, p. 7, 8, 11a, 11b, 13, 15a,
  16, 19a, 21, 26

"Slim Goodbody," "Squirt," and Render Ranch
illustrations, copyright © Slim Goodbody

Acknowledgements:
The author would like to thank the following
children for all their help in this project:
Lucas Burstein, Louisa Crane,
Isabella Crane, Aiden Gordon,
Ginny Laurita, Renaissance Lyman,
Yanmei McElhaney, Joshua Montavo

Library and Archives Canada Cataloguing in Publication

Burstein, John
    The exciting endocrine system : how do my glands
work? / John Burstein.

(Slim Goodbody's body buddies)
Includes index.
ISBN 978-0-7787-4418-4 (bound).--ISBN 978-0-7787-4432-0 (pbk.)

    1. Endocrine glands--Juvenile literature. I. Title.
II. Series: Burstein, John . Slim Goodbody's body buddies.

QP187.B87 2009   j612.4   C2009-900022-9

Library of Congress Cataloging-in-Publication Data

Burstein, John.
    Tthe exciting endocrine system : how do my glands work? / John
Burstein.
        p. cm. -- (Slim Goodbody's body buddies)
    Includes index.
    ISBN 978-0-7787-4432-0 (pbk. : alk. paper) -- ISBN 978-0-7787-4418-4
(reinforced lib. bdg. : alk. paper)
    1. Endocrine glands--Juvenile literature. 2. Endocrinology--Juvenile
literature. I. Title. II. Series.

    QP187.B87 2009
    612.4--dc22
                                              2008054460

Crabtree Publishing Company

www.crabtreebooks.com   1-800-387-7650

Copyright © **2009 CRABTREE PUBLISHING COMPANY.** All rights reserved. No part of this publication may be reproduced, stored in a retrieval system
or be transmitted in any form or by any means, electronic, mechanical, photocopying, recording, or otherwise, without the prior written permission of Crabtree
Publishing Company.

Published in Canada
Crabtree Publishing
616 Welland Ave.
St. Catharines, Ontario
L2M 5V6

Published in the United States
Crabtree Publishing
PMB16A
350 Fifth Ave., Suite 3308
New York, NY 10118

Published in the United Kingdom
Crabtree Publishing
White Cross Mills
High Town, Lancaster
LA1 4XS

Published in Australia
Crabtree Publishing
386 Mt. Alexander Rd.
Ascot Vale (Melbourne)
VIC 3032

About the Author
John Burstein (also known as Slim Goodbody) has been entertaining and educating children
for over thirty years. His programs have been broadcast on CBS, PBS, Nickelodeon, USA,
and Discovery. He has won numerous awards including the Parent's Choice Award and the
President's Council's Fitness Leader Award. Currently, Mr. Burstein tours the country with his
multimedia live show "Bodyology." For more information, please visit **slimgoodbody.com**.

CONTENTS

Words in **bold** are defined in the glossary on page 30.

Meet the Body Buddies

HELLO. MY NAME IS SLIM GOODBODY.

I am very happy that you are reading this book. It means that you want to learn about your body!

I believe that the more you know about how your body works, the prouder you will feel.

I believe that the prouder you feel, the more you will do to take care of yourself.

I believe that the more you do to take care of yourself, the happier and healthier you will be.

To provide you with the very best information about how your body works, I have put together a team of good friends. I call them my Body Buddies, and I hope they will become your Body Buddies, too!

Let me introduce them to you:

- **HUFF AND PUFF** will guide you through the lungs and the respiratory system.

- **TICKER** will lead you on a journey to explore the heart and circulatory system.

- **COGNOS** will explain how the brain and nervous system work.

- **SQUIRT** will let you in on the secrets of tiny glands that do big jobs.

- **FLEX AND STRUT** will walk you through the workings of your bones and muscles.

- **GURGLE** will give you a tour of the stomach and digestive system.

HUFF & PUFF Say...
YOUR RESPIRATORY SYSTEM IS MADE UP OF YOUR LUNGS, ALL THE AIRWAYS CONNECTED WITH THEM, AND THE MUSCLES THAT HELP YOU BREATHE.

TICKER Says...
YOUR CIRCULATORY SYSTEM IS MADE UP OF YOUR HEART, WHICH PUMPS YOUR BLOOD, AND THE TUBES, CALLED BLOOD VESSELS, THROUGH WHICH YOUR BLOOD FLOWS.

COGNOS Says...
YOUR NERVOUS SYSTEM IS MADE UP OF YOUR BRAIN, **SPINAL CORD**, AND ALL THE NERVES THAT RUN THROUGHOUT YOUR BODY.

SQUIRT Says...
YOUR ENDOCRINE SYSTEM IS MADE UP OF MANY DIFFERENT GLANDS THAT PRODUCE SUBSTANCES TO HELP YOUR BODY WORK RIGHT.

GURGLE Says...
YOUR DIGESTIVE SYSTEM HELPS TURN THE FOOD YOU EAT INTO ENERGY. IT INCLUDES YOUR STOMACH, LIVER, AND INTESTINES.

FLEX & STRUT Say...
YOUR MUSCULAR SYSTEM IS MADE UP OF MUSCLES THAT HELP YOUR BODY MOVE. THE SKELETAL SYSTEM IS MADE UP OF THE BONES THAT HOLD YOUR BODY UP.

LITTLE GIANTS

HELLO.

MY NAME IS SQUIRT. I AM A THYROID GLAND. I AM PART OF A SPECIAL TEAM CALLED THE ENDOCRINE SYSTEM. MOST OF MY TEAM MEMBERS ARE SMALL, BUT WE ALL HAVE BIG JOBS. I THINK OF US AS LITTLE GIANTS.

GLORIOUS GLANDS

Your endocrine system is made up of special groups of **cells** called glands. These glands include:

- The hypothalamus
- The pituitary
- The pineal
- The thyroid
- The parathyroids
- The adrenals
- The thymus
- The pancreas

The endocrine glands are located throughout your body and control different body functions.

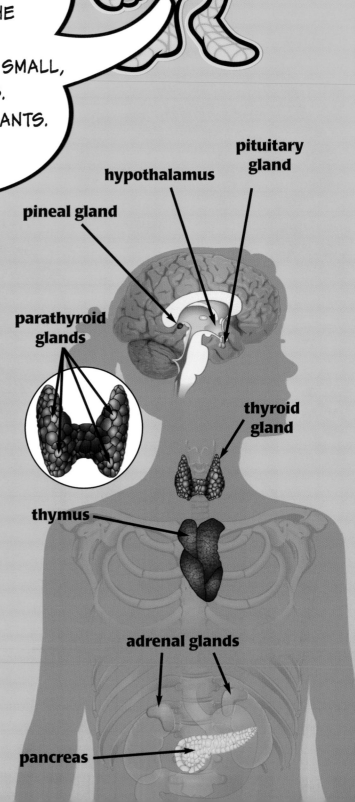

pituitary gland

hypothalamus

pineal gland

parathyroid glands

thyroid gland

thymus

adrenal glands

pancreas

COGNOS says...
YOUR NERVOUS SYSTEM AND ENDOCRINE SYSTEM OFTEN WORK TOGETHER TO HELP THE BODY FUNCTION PROPERLY.

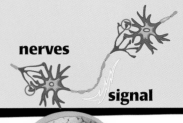

nerves

signal

brain

KINDS OF CONTROL

Your nervous system and your endocrine system work in different ways to help control body functions.

- Your brain sends tiny electrical message signals through the nerves. Each message reaches only certain cells.

- Your endocrine glands release special chemical messengers called **hormones**. Hormones travel through the bloodstream and are able to reach all of your cells.

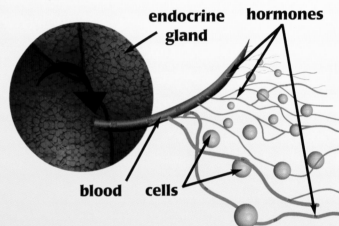

endocrine gland

hormones

blood   cells

KEEPING THE BALANCE

"Homeostasis" is a word that describes the normal, balanced, steady way your body works. For example:

- Your body temperature stays pretty much the same through the day.
- Your heart keeps a regular beat and does not jump from slow to fast for no reason.
- Your energy level does not rise and fall moment to moment.
- You grow gradually and do not sprout up five inches (13 cm) over night.

Your endocrine system plays a major role in maintaining homeostasis.

HORMONE FACTORY

ENDOCRINE GLANDS ARE LIKE FACTORIES. WE STAY BUSY MANUFACTURING, STORING, AND **SECRETING** CHEMICALS CALLED HORMONES.

MARVELOUS MESSENGERS

The word "hormone" comes from a Greek word meaning "I excite." This is a good name because hormones spark action in different parts of your body. Altogether, you have about 40 exciting hormones. They are busy helping control a wide variety of body activities, including these:

- Growth
- Strength
- Energy level
- Moods
- Hunger and thirst
- Body temperature
- Sleep

TICKER says... YOUR HEART WORKS HARD TO PUMP BLOOD. BLOOD CARRIES HORMONES THROUGH YOUR BODY.

HITTING THE TARGET

Hormones travel in the blood and can come in contact with every single one of your cells. However, each type of hormone can only affect certain kinds of cells. The cells a hormone can affect are called target cells.

endocrine gland

target cell

hormones

To understand how this works, imagine that each kind of target cell has its own kind of lock. Imagine that each type of hormone has its own type of key.

If the hormone key does not fit the cell lock, the hormone does not affect the cell.

If the hormone key fits, it gets into the target cell and sends chemical instructions that affect the inner workings of the cell.

STOP AND START

Hormones work in two ways:

1. Some hormones start activities in your body, such as growing.

2. Other hormones stop those activities.

If the endocrine system did not work this way, once something got started, there would be no stopping it. For example, you would never stop getting taller!

9

SLEEPY TIME

YOU CAN THANK YOUR PINEAL GLAND FOR HELPING YOU GET A GOOD NIGHT'S SLEEP.

FRONT AND CENTER

Your tiny pineal gland is only about the size of a pea. It is less than 0.3 inch (8 mm) long. That is a little less then the length of half your thumb. The pineal gland is located in the center of your brain, directly behind your eyes.

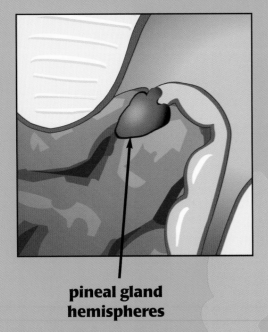

pineal gland hemispheres

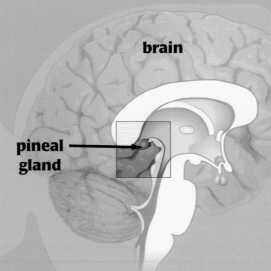

brain

pineal gland

GURGLE says...
THE PINE CONE-SHAPED PINEAL GLAND GETS ITS NAME FROM THE LATIN WORD "PINEA," WHICH MEANS "PINE CONE."

MELLOW MELATONIN

Your pineal gland secretes only one kind of hormone. The hormone is called melatonin. When melatonin is released, you start feeling sleepy. When there is a lot of melatonin in your blood, you stay asleep.

THE WAKE-SLEEP CYCLE

Scientists have discovered that the amount of light entering your eyes affects how much melatonin your pineal gland secretes. At night there is less light, and your pineal gland releases more melatonin. That is why you get tired at night. In the morning, the world gets

brighter and your pineal gland produces less melatonin and you start to wake up. This is called the wake-sleep cycle.

BE A SCIENTIST

You can explore the times you feel sleepy.

Directions:

1. During the next week, write down the time you start to feel sleepy.

2. During the same week, write down the time you wake up.

Do you start feeling sleepy when it gets dark outside? If you do, then you have your pineal gland to thank!

Here is what you will need:
- A paper
- A pen

A Grand Gland

THE HYPOTHALAMUS IS THE MAIN LINK BETWEEN THE ENDOCRINE SYSTEM AND THE NERVOUS SYSTEM.

IT IS ONE OF THE BUSIEST GLANDS.

HYPOTHALAMUS

The hypothalamus is a tiny gland located in the lower central part of the brain just above the brain stem. Information reaches the hypothalamus to let it know that changes are needed somewhere in the body. The hypothalamus then starts secreting hormones. These hormones travel to the pituitary gland located right below the hypothalamus.

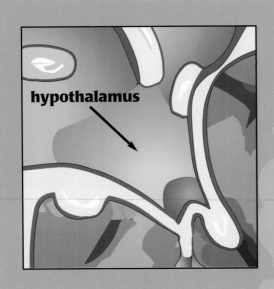

hypothalamus

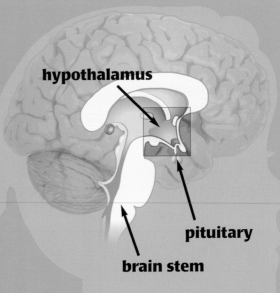

hypothalamus

pituitary

brain stem

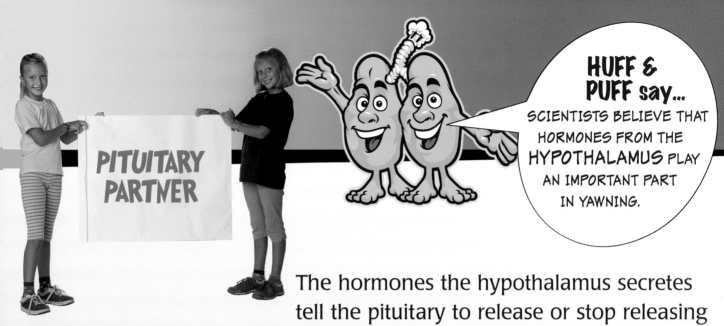

HUFF &
PUFF say...
SCIENTISTS BELIEVE THAT
HORMONES FROM THE
HYPOTHALAMUS PLAY
AN IMPORTANT PART
IN YAWNING.

PITUITARY
PARTNER

The hormones the hypothalamus secretes tell the pituitary to release or stop releasing hormones of its own. Pituitary hormones help control things such as body temperature, hunger, thirst, **blood pressure**, and **emotions**.

TEMPERATURE CONTROL

If your hypothalamus detects that you are getting too warm, it sends hormones to your pituitary gland. Here is what happens next:

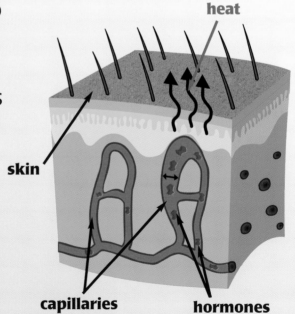

1. The pituitary sends hormones to the tiny blood vessels called capillaries, located in your skin.
2. The hormones tell the capillaries to get wider.
3. As the capillaries widen, more blood flows through them.
4. The flowing blood releases body heat through the surface of the skin.
5. Releasing body heat cools the body down.

If your body is getting too cold, other hormones are released that cause the capillaries in the skin to narrow. When this happens, the blood flow decreases near the surface of the skin, and body heat is kept in.

THE POWERFUL PITUITARY

THE PITUITARY IS SOMETIMES CALLED THE MASTER GLAND. THAT IS BECAUSE MOST OF THE OTHER GLANDS DEPEND ON PITUITARY HORMONES TO TELL US WHEN TO RELEASE HORMONES OF OUR OWN.

MASTER GLAND

Your pituitary is a small, oval-shaped gland located under the hypothalamus. It is about the size of a lima bean and weighs about 0.018 ounce (0.5 gram). The pituitary is connected to the hypothalamus by a stalk and is divided into two **lobes** that secrete different hormones:

1. The **anterior** lobe
2. The **posterior** lobe

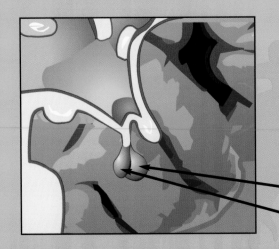

anterior pituitary
posterior pituitary

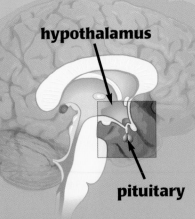

hypothalamus

pituitary

FLEX & STRUT say... THE PITUITARY GLAND ALSO RELEASES CHEMICALS CALLED ENDORPHINS. THESE CHEMICALS HELP REDUCE FEELINGS OF PAIN.

GET GROWING

The anterior lobe of your pituitary gland secretes a growth hormone that causes the cells in your bones and muscles to increase in size and in number. Growth hormones also make sure that cartilage is added to the ends of your bones. Cartilage helps make your bones longer and thicker. Once your body is finished growing, your pituitary sends only enough growth hormones to help maintain the size and strength of your bones and muscles.

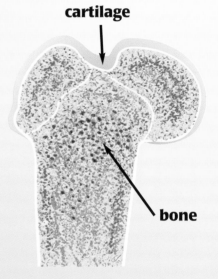

cartilage

bone

WATER WATCHER

The posterior lobe of the pituitary releases a hormone that helps keep enough water in your body. This hormone controls the amount of urine your kidneys release and the amount you sweat.

BE A SCIENTIST

It is fun to see how much you grow year by year.

Here is what you will need:
• A door frame
• A pencil
• Ten years

Directions:

1. Get your parents' permission to make small marks on a door frame.

2. Each year on your birthday, make a mark to show your height.

Year by year, the marks will show you how much you have grown and how your pituitary gland is working.

10 years

5 years

2 years

75

GERM BUSTER

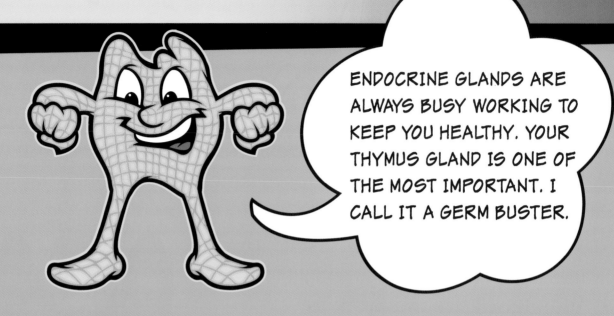

ENDOCRINE GLANDS ARE ALWAYS BUSY WORKING TO KEEP YOU HEALTHY. YOUR THYMUS GLAND IS ONE OF THE MOST IMPORTANT. I CALL IT A GERM BUSTER.

SMALL AND STRONG

Your thymus is a soft, flat, pinkish-gray gland in your chest. It is located behind your breast bone. Your thymus has two lobes. Each lobe is divided into smaller sections called lobules. Each lobule has an outer covering called a cortex and an inner center called the medulla. When you were born, your thymus gland weighed less than half an ounce (14 g). Your thymus will continue to grow until you reach your teen years. It will then weigh about 1.5 oz (42.5 g).

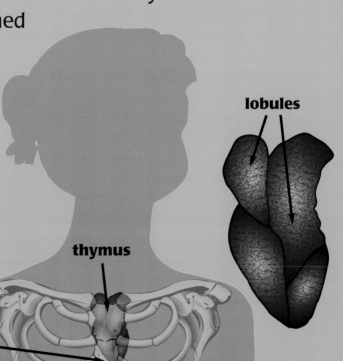

lobules

thymus

breast bone

TICKER says...
BLOOD CARRIES
T-CELLS THROUGHOUT
THE BODY TO FIGHT
INFECTION.

DEFEND YOURSELF

Your thymus gland helps fight disease. When germs invade, special blood cells called T-cells are sent to attack the germs before they cause real trouble.

The "T" in T-cells stands for thymus. Your thymus releases hormones that allow T-cells to increase in number both in the thymus itself and in other parts of the body.

AGING

As people grow older, the thymus gland begins to shrink. When the thymus shrinks, it produces fewer hormones and T-cell production goes down. This means that as people get older, their ability to fight disease decreases.

BE A SCIENTIST

Help your body fight disease.

Here is what you will need:
- A sink
- A bar of soap
- Your hands
- A towel
- A clock

Directions:

1. Using plenty of soap and water, scrub your hands.

2. Make sure you wash top and bottom and between all of your fingers and around your fingernails.

3. Keep washing for 20 seconds.

4. Rinse the soap away and dry your hands.

Keeping your hands clean prevents many germs from getting into your body in the first place.

AMAZING ADRENALS

WHEN YOU ARE FEELING SICK OR STRESSED OR WHEN YOU ARE IN A DANGEROUS SITUATION, BE GLAD YOU HAVE YOUR ADRENAL GLANDS.

TWO TRIANGLES

You have two adrenal glands that produce more than 30 different hormones. Each adrenal has a triangular shape and sits on top of a kidney. Each adrenal weighs less than one ounce (28.3 g) and has two parts with different responsibilities:

1. The adrenal medulla controls how your body responds to stress.

2. The adrenal cortex helps control how energy is stored, how your kidneys work, and many other body functions.

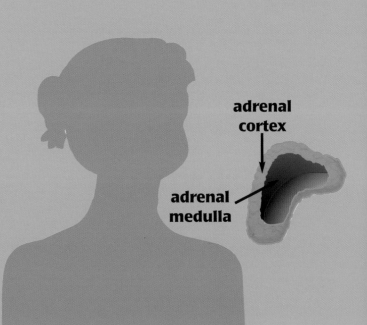

adrenal cortex

adrenal medulla

adrenal glands

kidneys

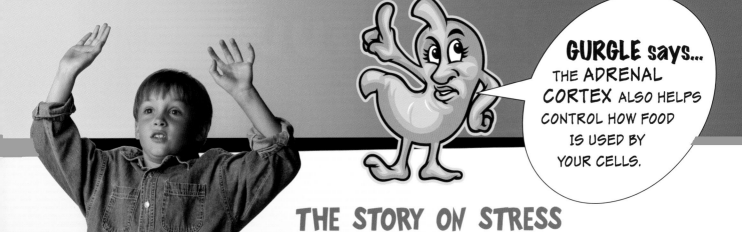

THE STORY ON STRESS

Stress is the feeling you get when you are worried, scared, sick, or uncomfortable. Dangerous situations also cause stress. Stress actually changes the way your body works. It can make your muscles feel tight, your hair stand up on end, and your stomach feel queasy.

STRESS BUSTER

In times of stress, your adrenal medulla secretes a hormone called adrenalin. Adrenalin can increase your strength and mental alertness by doing these things:

- Speeding up your **heart rate**.
- Increasing the amount of blood your heart pumps with each beat.
- Widening the airways in your lungs so you can get more oxygen.
- Increasing the blood flow to your muscles so you can move faster.
- Increasing the blood flow to your brain so you can think more clearly.
- Helping to release food energy to your cells so you have more power.
- Widening the pupils of your eyes so you can see better.

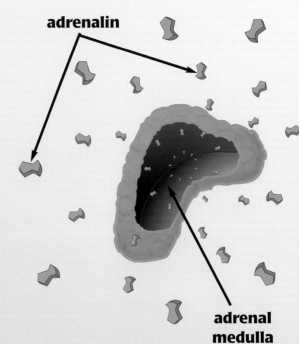

adrenalin

adrenal medulla

THE POWERFUL PANCREAS

YOUR POWERFUL PANCREAS IS RESPONSIBLE FOR MANY IMPORTANT JOBS. READ ON AND FIND OUT MORE.

BIGGER THAN THE REST

Your pancreas is about six to seven inches (15–17.8 cm) long, which makes it the largest member of the endocrine system. The pancreas is located behind your stomach and stretches across the back of your abdomen. Your pancreas contains small groups of cells called islets of Langerhans, or islets. Islets produce several different hormones. Two of the most important of these hormones are:

1. Insulin
2. Glucogon

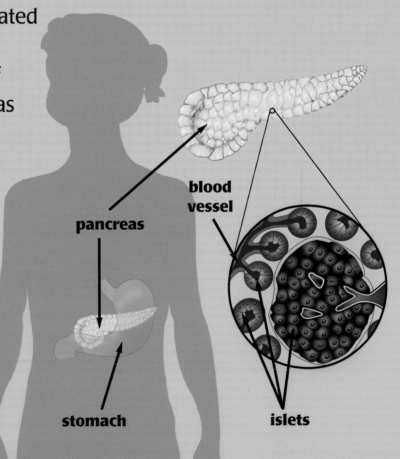

pancreas

blood vessel

stomach

islets

GURGLE says... YOUR PANCREAS DOES MORE THAN RELEASE ENDOCRINE HORMONES. IT ALSO HELPS THE DIGESTIVE SYSTEM BREAK DOWN FOOD.

BODY FUEL

When you eat or drink, much of your food is broken down into a simple sugar called glucose. Glucose is sometimes called "blood sugar." Glucose is fuel for your cells, just as gas is fuel for a car.

INCREDIBLE INSULIN

Your blood carries glucose to all your cells, but glucose cannot get into your cells all by itself. Glucose needs a helper. That helper is insulin. Insulin is a hormone that your pancreas secretes. Insulin allows glucose to enter your cells. Once enough glucose enters the cells, your blood sugar level drops and your pancreas slows down or stops the release of insulin.

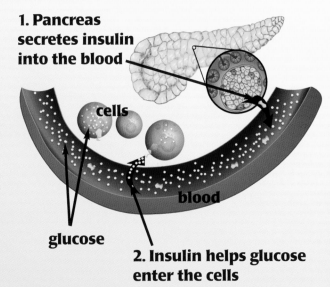

1. Pancreas secretes insulin into the blood

cells

blood

glucose

2. Insulin helps glucose enter the cells

GLORIOUS GLUCOGON

Any leftover glucose that is not needed by your cells is sent to your liver for storage. Later, if the levels of glucose in your blood fall too low, your pancreas secretes another hormone. It is called glucagon. Glucagon is sent to your liver and causes it to release the sugar it has stored up. The sugar re-enters your blood and can be used by your cells.

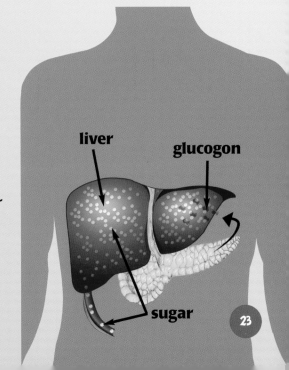

liver

glucogon

sugar

23

THE ENDOCRINE SYSTEM

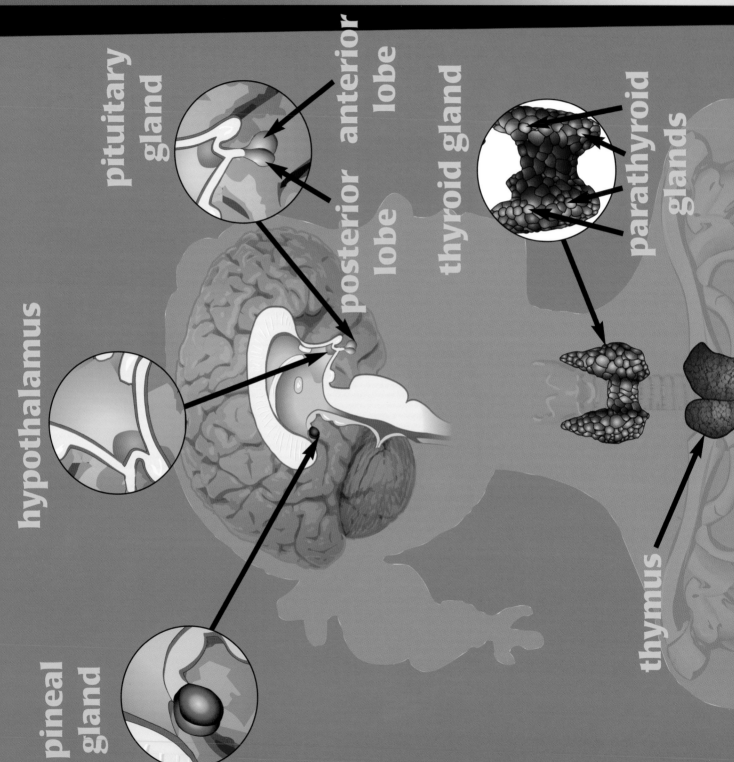

pituitary gland

anterior lobe

posterior lobe

thyroid gland

parathyroid glands

hypothalamus

pineal gland

thymus

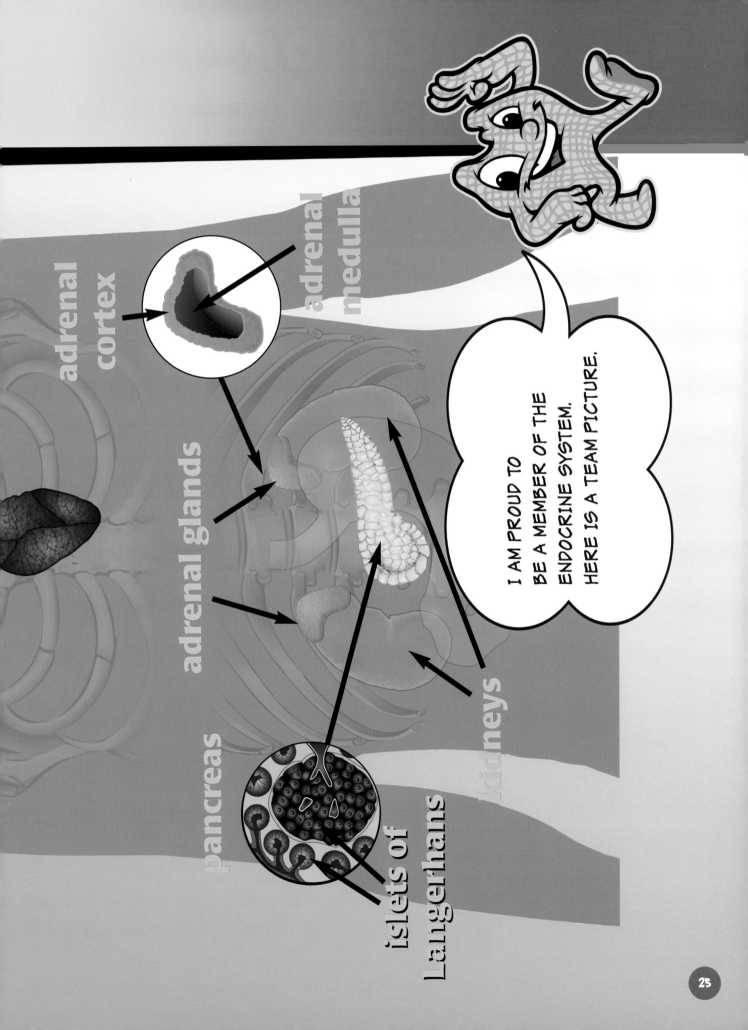

Too Much or Too Little

ENDOCRINE GLANDS WORK HARD TO KEEP YOU HEALTHY, BUT SOMETIMES WE SECRETE TOO MANY HORMONES — OR TOO FEW. THE WRONG AMOUNT OF HORMONES CAN LEAD TO TROUBLE.

DARK MOOD

During the winter months, when days are shorter, some people develop a problem called SAD. SAD stands for "seasonal affective disorder." When there is less light, sometimes the pineal gland produces too much melatonin. The extra melatonin causes people to feel very tired and unhappy.

Bright light reduces melatonin production, so doctors suggest that people with SAD stay in rooms with a special kind of bright light for several hours a day. This treatment often helps solve the problem of feeling sad from SAD!

COGNOS says... THE SPECIAL DOCTORS WHO DEAL WITH THE ENDOCRINE SYSTEM ARE CALLED **ENDOCRINOLOGISTS.**

DESTRUCTIVE DIABETES

When insulin is not being produced or when insulin cannot be used properly, glucose builds up in the blood. A high glucose level in the blood makes people sick.

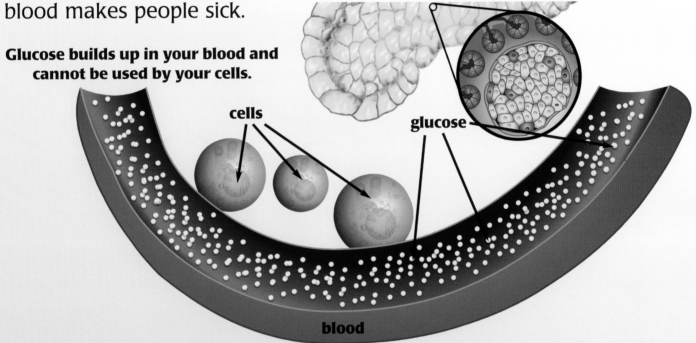

Glucose builds up in your blood and cannot be used by your cells.

cells

glucose

blood

If diabetes is not treated, it can lead to serious kidney problems, nerve damage, blindness, and early heart disease.

DEALING WITH DIABETES

There are two main types of diabetes. People with type 1 diabetes need to treat their disease with regular injections of insulin. People with type 2 diabetes may also need insulin injections, but sometimes a healthy diet and plenty of exercise can help instead.

FABULOUS PHRASES

EACH SENTENCE IN THIS GAME IS MISSING A WORD THAT TELLS YOU SOMETHING ABOUT YOUR ENDOCRINE SYSTEM. THE MISSING WORD STARTS WITH THE SAME SOUND AS THE WORD IN CAPITAL LETTERS. CAN YOU FIGURE OUT WHAT THAT WORD MIGHT BE? FOR EXAMPLE, IF SENTENCE NUMBER ONE IS "SENDING HORMONES TO YOUR PITUITARY GLAND IS YOUR_____" YOU WOULD CHOOSE THE WORD "HYPOTHALAMUS." GOT IT?

The right words are upside down on the bottom of the page. If you cannot think of a word, you can find the answer on the page listed by the sentence.

1. Sending HORMONES to your pituitary gland is your _____. (clue: page 12)

2. HORMONES help keep your body functions regular by maintaining _____ (clue: page 7)

3. Many scientists say that the most POWERFUL gland in your body is the _____. (clue: page 14)

4. The melatonin hormone that helps PUT you to sleep is secreted by your _____ gland. (clue: page 11)

5. If your calcium level drops too low, certain hormones will be PRODUCED by your _____. (clue: page 17)

6. You would not grow TALLER without the hormones secreted by your _____. (clue: page 16)

7. Your germ fighting T-CELLS are secreted by your _____. (clue: page 19)

8. Your adrenal glands secrete a hormone that helps your heart increase its PUMPING _____. (clue: page 21)

| A. Thyroid | C. Hypothalamus | E. Parathyroids | E. Power |
| B. Pineal | D. Pituitary | F. Thymus | F. Homeostasis |

ANSWERS: 1-C, 2-H, 3-D, 4-B, 5-E, 6-A, 7-F, 8-G

Amazing Facts About Your Endocrine System

AN ANCIENT GREEK DOCTOR WROTE ABOUT THE PINEAL GLAND ALMOST 2,000 YEARS AGO!

PEOPLE WITH TOO LITTLE OR TOO MUCH GROWTH HORMONE GROW IN UNUSUAL WAYS. THEY CAN EITHER STAY VERY SHORT OR GROW TO BE SUPER TALL.

FEVERS ARE CONTROLLED BY THE HYPOTHALAMUS.

CHILDREN UNDER SEVEN YEARS OF AGE PRODUCE MORE MELATONIN THAN OLDER CHILDREN AND ADULTS.

THE HIGHEST BODY TEMPERATURE EVER RECORDED WAS 115.7 DEGREES F (46.5 DEGREES C.)

ROMAN EMPERORS BELIEVED THAT EATING LETTUCE WOULD HELP A PERSON SLEEP.

THE AVERAGE DURATION OF A YAWN IS ABOUT SIX SECONDS.

FOR MANY YEARS, SCIENTISTS BELIEVED THE THYMUS WAS A TOTALLY USELESS GLAND.

THE FIRST TIME THE TERM HYPOTHALAMUS WAS USED WAS IN 1895.

TABLE SALT CONTAINS IODINE TO HELP KEEP YOUR THYROID HEALTHY.

RENE DESCARTES, A 17TH-CENTURY FRENCH MATHEMATICIAN, BELIEVED THE SOUL RESIDED IN THE PINEAL GLAND.

Glossary

anterior Closer to the front of something, especially the body

blood pressure The pressure, or force, of your blood against the walls of your blood vessels; too much or too little pressure can mean that your heart is working either too hard or not hard enough to pump blood to all the parts of your body

calcium A special substance, called a mineral, that is important for building strong bones and helping your nerves and muscles work well

cells The smallest units, or structures, that make up the body; cells are so tiny that they cannot be seen without a microscope

emotions How you feel about things

heart rate The number of times your heart beats in a certain amount of time, usually a minute

hormones Substances produced by the body's glands and transported, or delivered, to various parts of the body, usually through the blood; hormones help regulate, or control many of the body's functions, such as growth, burning up fat, and fighting disease

infection The attack of healthy parts of your body by germs; infections can lead to injury or disease; they should be cleaned and treated with medicine

isthmus A narrow passage or piece of tissue connecting two larger organs or body parts; in geography, an isthmus is a narrow strip of land connecting two larger land masses

lobes Parts or sections of something, either divided into segments, like the lobes of the hypothalamus or brain, or hanging, like earlobes

posterior Closer to the rear or back of something, especially the body

secreting Producing and discharging, or letting loose, a substance, such as a hormone

spinal cord The cord of nerve tissues running down the center of the backbone

FOR MORE INFORMATION

BOOKS

The Endocrine System (Human Body Systems). Stephanie Watson and Kelli Miller. Greenwood Press.

Endocrine System (The Amazing Human Body). Lorrie Klosterman. Marshall Cavendish Children's Books.

The Endocrine System (Human Body Systems). Rebecca Olien. Capstone Press.

The Endocrine System (The Human Body, How It Works). Lynette Rushton. Chelsea House Publishers.

WEBSITES

CDC Department of Health and Human Services: BAM: Body and Mind.
www.bam.gov/sub_yourbody/yourbody_diabetes.html
Learn more about diabetes and its treatment and prevention.

Discovery Kids: Your Gross and Cool Body
yucky.discovery.com/flash/body/pg000133.html
This website has lots of information and very cool "yucky" interactive games to play.

Human Anatomy Online
www.innerbody.com/image/endoov.html
Take an interactive tour to learn more about the endocrine glands.

Kidshealth
kidshealth.org/kid/htbw/endocrine.html
Check out this website for a ton of information about your endocrine system and diabetes.

Slim Goodbody
www.slimgoodbody.com
Discover loads of fun and free downloads for kids, teachers, and parents.

INDEX

Printed in the U.S.A. - CG